BOSTON

CITY OF MANY DREAMS

First English edition published by Colour Library Books Ltd.
© 1984 Illustrations and text: Colour Library Books Ltd.,
 Guildford, Surrey, England.
This edition published by Crescent Books.
h g f e d c b a
Display and filmsetting by Acesetters Ltd., Richmond,
 Surrey, England.
Colour separations by Llovet, S.A., Barcelona, Spain.
Printed by **SIRVENSAE**, Bound by Eurobinder, Barcelona, Spain
ISBN 0-517-43637X
CRESCENT 1984

BOSTON

CITY OF MANY DREAMS

Text by Bill Harris

Produced by
TED SMART and DAVID GIBBON

CRESCENT BOOKS

A few years ago, inspired by the success of the British TV series *Upstairs Downstairs*, CBS Television produced a series of its own called *Beacon Hill*.

The setting was Boston in the 1920s, and no expense was spared to make it historically accurate. Costumes were checked and rechecked with museum collections. Accents were refined to be just right. Antiques were brought in at great expense. The series was even filmed right on Beacon Hill, using exteriors at 89 Mount Vernon Street, one of the only houses on the Hill that isn't shoehorned in among its neighbors; the only one with a broad driveway.

But that wasn't the only thing that was different about TV's *Beacon Hill*. The story was about an upwardly-mobile Irish family in the 1920s; any time before, or any time since, right up until the last twenty years or so, Irish families simply didn't live there.

Beacon Hill was the center of Boston society almost from the beginning when a silversmith named Paul Revere, a lawyer named James Otis, an importer named John Hancock and the richest man in the whole colony, Thomas Boylston, built small mansions there to take advantage of the view.

Today it's a neighborhood of steep, narrow streets lined with townhouses, many of which have long since been subdivided into very high-priced apartments. Some ground floor shops are rented by sandal makers and poster dealers, galleries and handicraft stores. Interspersed among them, occasional mansions designed by Charles Bulfinch, who gets credit for the State House and just about every other very important building in town, are still occupied by some of the Old Families. And along with them, Beacon Hill is still a symbol of wealth and privilege, a place from which one can look down on the rabble and over to the State House for help in keeping the rabble in their place.

The upwardly-mobile Irish of the 20s, it should be mentioned, found their place outside Boston, in suburbs like Brookline, Dorchester and Jamaica Plain.

Most of the houses on Beacon Hill were in place and occupied by people with a high idea of their place in life before Irish immigrants began arriving in huge numbers in the early 19th century. Mount Vernon Street, where the television series was filmed, is one of the best on the Hill and an absolute joy for strollers. It's a happy mix of Classical and Federal architecture with a little sprinkling of Victorian just to keep you smiling. Each building, not just on this street, but all over the Hill, has a personality of its own. But together they're like a Vivaldi concerto with the State House a virtuoso solo instrument.

Wrought-iron fences and balconies soften stone and brick; gas lights make shadows dance. In summer, red geraniums and green ivy spill out of window boxes. In winter, especially at Christmas, the light and warmth comes at you through high mullioned windows. It's city life as city life was meant to be!

One of the houses on the Hill is a little lower than the rest because the lot it stands on had been owned by the man across the street who made it a condition of the sale that no structure on it could be more than 13 feet high. After all, anything higher would spoil his view. Down the block, the seller of some lots made the buyer agree to set the buildings back off the street so he wouldn't be blocked from his view of the Charles River. Who could blame either of them? But where in the world but Boston could you find buyers who would agree to such demands?

John Hancock's house on the Hill was torn down some years ago and replaced by another, whose owners took their old address from down the street. The Architectural Commission would have saved it today, but when it was offered for sale to the state as a landmark, it was turned down because the price was too high.

Not far from the site is the Boston Athenaeum, one of the world's great libraries. Among other things, it contains George Washington's personal book collection, each with Washington's book plate and his signature. It's a strictly private library, founded by Daniel Webster and others, including Ralph Waldo Emerson's father, open only to the gentlemen who support it and the scholars who need it.

Gentlemen and scholars! The words go with Boston as easily as clams go with beer!

It wasn't always the case. Back in 1624, not long after the Pilgrims had settled themselves down in Plymouth, a ship full of indentured servants arrived in Massachusetts Bay. Their leader, Thomas Morton, freed them and invited them to settle down with him in a town he called Merriemount. They were all from Elizabethan England and had quite different ideas about life from the Puritans who preceded them. They loved a good time. They thought it was great fun to go fishing and hunting and not do much else. As a result, the Indians adored them.

They hadn't been there three years when Morton decided it was time they had a big party. After all, hadn't the Pilgrims put together a three-day feast at harvest time a few years before? May Day was the day he picked, and as a centerpiece for the party, they built an 80-foot maypole topped with deer antlers. Then the fun began. William Bradford, of Plymouth, said in his *History* that they were "drinking and dancing about it many days together, inviting the Indean woman for their consorts, dancing and frisking togither like so many faeries, and worse practices." Sounds like more fun than Thanksgiving? Shame on you!

It was all too much for the long-suffering Plymouth Puritans. But they were a peaceful lot, and they held their peace. Then it was discovered that the Merriemount settlers were selling guns to the Indians. The Puritans dispatched a force under the command of one Captain Miles Standish to drive them back where they came from.

They ordered Morton to surrender, but he hurled back an insult instead, calling poor little Miles Standish "Captain Shrimpe." Standish attacked and easily defeated them. They were soon loaded on a passing ship and sent back to England. Standish admitted later the defeat was easy because they were "over armed with drinke."

And so, thanks to the Demon Rum, Massachusetts Bay was made safe for God-fearing people. And it wouldn't be long before they arrived.

The settlers who followed were Puritans, like the people who had built the colony at Plymouth. But not exactly the same. In Plymouth, their brand of Puritanism removed them completely from the Church of England, which they felt was far too Roman. The new breed felt the same, but believed they should remain Anglicans and work from within to change the church.

They formed a company called the Massachusetts Bay Company, which was chartered to settle and to trade, with a heavy emphasis on the latter. They arrived in the summer of 1629 and settled in a place they called Salem, meaning "house of peace."

Up until that time, most of the American colonies were run by trading companies headquartered in London. The directors of the Massachusetts Bay Company, apparently believing their own P.R., decided to move themselves to America, too. That way, they had less interference from the Crown and the Church back home. It gave them control over their own destiny.

And so, in 1630, John Winthrop, Lord of Groton Manor and head of the Massachusetts Bay Company, arrived in Salem with 400 settlers and an urge to take over. Rather than settling in Salem, which was already overcrowded, they moved down the bay and established a string of settlements, one of which they called Boston.

Within the next ten years, another 20,000 followed them!

Winthrop's brand of Puritanism attracted middle and upper-class businessmen, who sold out their interests back home and, as a result, arrived with some cash in their pockets. "Send us your poor..." was not a slogan the Massachusetts Bay Company would have used. The newcomers' cash bought food and housing and then went back to England to pay for things they needed but couldn't produce for themselves. Also, because they were businessmen, it was only natural they should stick to their last in the new country. In no time at all, they were trading fish for Virginia tobacco and shipping it off to England. They were shipping fish to Portugal and coming back loaded with wine. They had established themselves as princes. And that made them the Establishment in colonial America. Gentlemen to the core, and scholars, of course. One of the first things they learned was that rum was in great demand in Africa. And that Africans were in great demand in the West Indies, which is where the sugar comes from to make rum. They got the message, and for a long time Boston produced more rum than any city in the world.

But that's not to say that scholarship in Boston was only restricted to chasing money. The Puritans believed that anyone who couldn't read was, at the very least, Satan's tool, and most likely doomed to damnation and hellfire. To prevent it, one of their first acts was to build a school in Boston, modelled after the ones they knew in England. They called it the Boston Latin School, and it became the model for public education all over the United States. The idea was to teach youngsters to read the Bible for themselves so they wouldn't have to get the Word by hearsay. It was only for boys, mind you. Not that they didn't want to keep their daughters from the Devil's clutches; but most girls could learn to read at their mother's knee, while they were learning needlepoint and all those other essential arts. If mom was too busy, and the family rich enough, there were private schools for girls, and they taught social dancing along with reading and writing.

The Massachusetts Bay people were even more concerned about the future of their church than the future of their children, and fretted about what might happen if the supply of preachers ran out. Every town needed one, and there were plenty of good men in England who wanted the jobs. But in the long run, they knew they had better develop some home-grown product.

One of the preachers brought over from England was a man named John Harvard, who died within a year of arriving. He was so impressed by the idea of establishing a college that he left his library and half his fortune, about £400, in his will to get the ball rolling. It impressed the colonists enough to name the place after him, and the General Court enough to match his grant out of tax receipts.

The new college was established in a place called Newtown. But, probably as a gesture to give it confidence and a tradition to live up to, they quickly changed the name to Cambridge.

John Harvard wouldn't recognize the place today, any more than he'd recognize himself in the wonderful, but not historically accurate, statue of him by Daniel Chester French. The old town common is partly preserved in Harvard Square, but new buildings of just about every period have taken up the space that was originally left between the houses. A great many fine colonial buildings still stand in Cambridge, but even the oldest is some 50 years younger than Harvard itself. And a great many buildings that look colonial may have been built when your grandfather was a boy. Some of the buildings are Victorian, many are Gothic. It all depends on what was in style when they were built.

The oldest building on the Harvard campus is the Georgian Massachusetts Hall, built in 1718, and its mate, Harvard Hall, built about 50 years later. They faced the Cambridge Common until the 1880s, when Stanford White built Johnson Gate and the fence that goes with it. All the great architects seem to have contributed to the Harvard Campus. Charles Bulfinch's University Hall, Ware and Van Brunt's landmark Memorial Hall, H.H. Richardson's masterpiece Sever Hall, Horace Trumbauer's Widener Library, McKim, Mead & White's Robinson Hall and William Morris Hunt's Hunt Hall are all monuments to men who gave the country style. The great, 20th-century builders are represented here, too. Walter Gropius led the way and Cambridge is dotted with the work of such men as Edward D. Stone, Philip Johnson, I.M. Pei, Hugh Stubbins and others.

The first major reinforced concrete structure ever built is at Harvard, but it wasn't built by a modern architect. It's the Harvard Stadium, built in 1903 on an idea of Ira Nelson Hollis, a Harvard engineering professor.

Those big, white buildings you see when you cross Harvard Bridge from Boston to Cambridge aren't Harvard buildings at all, but part of another institution any city would be proud of, Massachusetts Institute of Technology. A few of its buildings reflect the Beaux Arts style that was popular when MIT moved over from

Boston in 1913, but most of it has the modern look of the work of men like Eduardo Catalano, Hugh Stubbins, Pietro Belluschi and Emery Roth. It's what goes on inside those buildings that's really important. Much of the atom bomb development and other technology of the Second World War happened here, and many of the ideas that put men on the moon came from the MIT scientists. Most important for all the rest of New England is that the brainpower centered in Cambridge attracts industry to the area in the form of companies who need to have a jump on all the latest developments.

But Harvard is where tradition lives. And some of the traditions leave outsiders scratching their heads. Back in the 19th century, it was a rule there that "no scholar shall go out of his chamber without coate, gown or cloake; and it should be modest and sober habit without strange ruffian-like or newfangled fashions, without any lavish dresse or excess of apparrell whatsoever."

From that came a rule that no freshman could wear his hat in Harvard Yard "unless it rains, hails or snows, provided he be on foot and have not both hands full."

Until recently, another tradition was that Harvard was for men only. Women, you see, enrolled in Radcliffe. They were taught by Harvard professors and Harvard's president signed their diplomas, which always bore the Harvard seal. Radcliffe and Harvard finally "got married," and a Radcliffe girl is as much a Harvard man as anybody.

On the other side of town, Boston has a tradition that goes back to the 1770s but is as new as the 1970s. Its centerpiece is a meat market called Faneuil Hall (pronounce it like flannel), which was one of the places a bunch of hotheads used as a secret meeting place to plan a revolution a little more than 200 years ago. The area it's in is called Dock Square, and it's not far from the place where some of those hotheads dumped a lot of British tea into the harbor just before their revolutionary plans went into action.

It was the city's marketplace from the very earliest times. That's where the ships were, and people knew they could eliminate the middleman if they did their dealing right on the docks. Over the years, other markets joined the original to handle the overflow, and the most elaborate of them, Quincy Market, has recently been restored in a $20 million effort that took six years. The restoration has given Boston the best waterfront area east of San Francisco. It's an exciting combination of food shops and restaurants, merchants selling plants and cookware, books and kitchenware, wine, cheese and whatever else can be sold to a crowd of people with not much more on their mind than enjoying themselves.

The setting is a 550-foot-long, narrow building with a three-story copper rotunda in the middle. Pushcart vendors on the wide brick plazas on each side are protected by glass awnings that keep the weather out, but let the sunshine in. About the only thing that's missing, compared to other restored historic neighborhoods around the country, are the poster sellers, the candle dealers, the head shops and incense peddlers. But nobody really seems to miss them much. Like so many other things about Boston, it's a civilized place.

Civilization reaches another great height in Boston's Back Bay. Lewis Mumford said it is "the outstanding achievement in American urban planning for the 19th century."

The Esplanade along the river gives its residents a place to get a breath of fresh air; the residential streets are separate from shopping streets, but not so separate as to hinder convenience; and there are commercial districts, too, so Back Bay people don't have to travel far to work. It's a neighborhood that includes McKim, Mead and White's magnificent Symphony Hall at one end, and the wonderful Public Gardens at the other. It includes Copley Square and Commonwealth Avenue, too. What city wouldn't be pleased to have either one?

The Boston Public Library is on Copley Square. McKim, Mead & White designed the original. Philip Johnson "improved" on their work in an addition he designed in 1972. Others have tried to improve Back Bay in recent years, too. The Prudential Life Insurance Company, for instance, built a complex of buildings in the 1960s that are probably best forgotten, except that the tower is so huge you can't escape it. Another insurance company, John Hancock, added its contribution with a 60-story tower. Its architect, who is probably better left nameless, envisioned an "invisible building" covered with a reflecting glass skin. Unfortunately, variable temperatures and high winds shattered the dream, and if Bostonians valued their lives they stayed away from the "windswept plaza" at the base. If they didn't get hit by flying glass, they got in the way of the sweepers. The windows that were blown out were replaced by plywood panels as a temporary measure, and the building was known as the plywood tower. The problems seem to have been corrected by now, but it's probably a good idea to make sure your life insurance is paid up if you plan to walk anywhere near it.

The Back Bay really was a bay when Winthrop and his company arrived. Or rather it was more like a marsh. As the city grew, some of the inlets were filled, but in the middle of the last century it was a mess. In 1857 the City Fathers built a special railroad over to Needham, and until the turn of the century trains went back and forth over it carrying dirt to fill in the bay. When the project was finished, people began to come down from Beacon Hill and across the Common to settle there. The Charles Street edge of the Common, all the way to Washington Street, had been the shoreline up until then. New streets like Commonwealth Avenue, which could have been imported from Paris, added to the lure of the latest thing. By the middle of the 19th century, anyone who wanted to be considered fashionable in Boston (and, after all, what else was there to aspire to?), just *had* to be seen walking on Commonwealth Avenue on the way from church to a stroll through the Commons.

The Boston Common is the oldest public park in the country. It was also the object of one of the first shrewd business deals by Puritans in America. When they arrived, the whole Shawmut Peninsula, where they built Boston, was owned by a preacher who was operating on a King's grant, and had lived there for nearly ten years. As a man of God, he was happy to see these God-fearing people from the old country and he invited them to stay. They took over. Oh, they were generous to him. They let him keep 50 acres, plenty of

land for a man who wasn't even a farmer. Within a few months, just to make things legal, they asked him to sell them his 50 acres. He did, gladly, for £30. But the deed he signed gave Winthrop and his company the whole peninsula. Sure, it was a low price. But even considering the value of the English pound today, it was a better deal than Peter Minuit gave the owners of Manhattan Island.

Everyone in the Colony was assessed to raise the money and, in return, the Governor decreed that the preacher's garden would henceforth be common property. And he was as good as his word. It still is.

At first, it was used as a pasture for the colonists' cows and a parade ground for their militia. Not much later, it was used for public executions and punishments of one sort or another. As in England at the time, a good hanging was a great crowd-pleaser. In Boston they called it going to see someone "turned off." It was also considered great fun to stroll along the Common and toss rotten eggs at some poor soul who had been sentenced to "an hour in ye stocks." Oddly, the first person to use the stocks in Boston was the unfortunate carpenter who built them. The Elders thought his price was too high for the work, so they fined him the amount of his bill and locked him up for an hour.

British troops were billeted on the Common, and left from there to try to beat Paul Revere to Lexington and Concord. Some of them, like those hanged, are buried under it.

Though the Boston Massacre, one of the first brushes with the British before the war, took place over on State Street, the memorial to its victims is on the Common. They say it's good luck to shake the hand of Crispus Attucks, the black man who was the first to give his life for his country in the Revolutionary War. If it's true, there are a lot of lucky people in Boston. The hand is the best-polished piece of bronze in the city.

They say the game of football was first played on the Boston Common. It was also the place where, in 1688, an event took place that would become a political football later. Goody Glover was hanged as a witch because she had been caught saying the rosary in Gaelic in front of a "craven image" of the Virgin. All Irishmen were devils. Everyone in Boston believed that in 1688.

One of the things that makes Boston, and all New England for that matter, unique in America is that it existed for two centuries, and more, with only a single culture. All the English colonies to the south welcomed anybody and everybody no matter where they came from. The Dutch were the originals in New York; Germans had flocked to Philadelphia; the French and Spanish were part of the established fabric almost everywhere. But Boston was quite content to stay English. In the first 20 years of the colony, some 20,000 people migrated there, and just about all of them came from England. Not only that, but almost all of them were Puritans dedicated with all their hearts to success, to God and to hard work (not necessarily in that order!).

As their numbers grew, so did the number of towns they lived in. But Boston was always at the heart of it, and no one ever dared challenge that. Later, as they began to industrialize, the great Boston entrepreneurs looked out into the countryside and, where the poets among them saw laughing, bubbling brooks and sparkling waterfalls, they saw free energy. They changed old towns and built new ones, and for the first time farmers didn't have to feel guilty over not having enough work to do in the wintertime. There was cloth to be woven, shoes to be made. There was work to be done.

There was so much work in fact, they needed more people to do it all. Then, as He had done so often in their view, God provided them with an answer to the problem. In 1845, Ireland was visited by a famine that wiped out more than a million people in less than five years. Rather than starve, a million and a half of them left the country. In spite of what they may have thought of old England, New England was very attractive indeed. There were jobs and opportunities there.

Within forty years, Boston had an Irish Mayor.

But what a terrible forty years it was! It was bad enough that these newcomers were Irish. One of Boston's venerable leaders wrote: "They were the scum of creation, beaten men from beaten races, representing the worst failure in the struggle for existence...These immigrants were inferior peoples whose prolific issue threatened the very foundations of Anglo-American civilization." That was part of the rub! These new immigrants were almost all Catholics. That was what the Puritans came to Boston to get away from. And with their views on birth control...well, it's only a matter of time, isn't it?

The Puritans called them "muckers" and "micks," "blacklegs" and "greenhorns." They hired their women, whom they always called "Bridget" at best, or "Biddy" at worst, to do the dirty work in their homes for $1.50 a week. Then they kept a third to pay for the board.

By the time the Irish arrived, the North End had already lost its cachet for the fashionable Yankees, and whole neighborhoods there had simply been abandoned. Irish families moved into the big, old mansions, usually one to a room, which meant they shared what sanitary facilities there were among dozens of whole families. And that, in turn, meant many of them fell victim to cholera, smallpox and worse.

But if the Puritans thought they were the only people God gave gifts to, they didn't know much about God or the Irish. One of the newcomers' gifts was for survival. They believed, as an article of faith, that a man's reward was in heaven. That helped them endure hardships even the toughest Yankee would have blanched at, because the Puritans believed just as strongly in the here and now, and that hardship was as much a punishment as a test.

The Irish had a gift for politics, too, and they knew how to use it. As a countermeasure, the Puritans set up residency laws and literacy laws to keep them from voting. But it was only a matter of time before that trick wouldn't work any more. They used their influence to spread stories that the Irish were nothing but drunkards, people who preferred welfare to an honest day's work and, worst of all, people who couldn't be loyal to any state because any information entrusted to them would be transmitted straight back to the Pope in Rome.

The old line leaders were, by and large, Republican in those days after the Civil War. So the Irish were Democrats. To counter that, Bostonians formed new parties that allowed them tighter control. One of them was called "The Know-Nothings," because its members usually didn't discuss what they stood for except with insiders.

They got to be so powerful that they elected a Governor, and gained control of both the state house and the city council in a single election. It was then people discovered how little they really did know. Though they did all they could to keep the Irish down, patience won out, and eventually the door was open for them to play the game they love so much: running for office and getting elected.

On the other side of the coin, if the established Bostonians had gone to the docks to meet the Irish with brass bands and CARE Packages, there still would have been trouble. The Irish had some experience with the "Bloody British" back home, and their new hosts were, in many cases, more British than their cousins back

home in Sussex. Even though without them America might have stayed a part of the British Empire to this day, they were English and proud of it. Then there was that problem of religion. To the Irish, being Protestant was much worse than being a heathen. And, of course, the Puritans were Protestants to a fault. It wasn't the first time and, unfortunately, not the last, that men used the love of God to justify hate.

By the time the Irish had gotten political clout, Boston had become different again. While all the scrapping was going on, Italians began arriving, then Lithuanians and Poles. Germans came, too, along with Portuguese, Scandinavians and French Canadians. But the Irish controlled the wards, and if you wanted a street light or a city job you had to go to them. And, after all those years of feeling the stings of prejudice, guess who was dealing them out. Human nature is a mysterious thing.

But no matter what else Boston immigrants found, most eventually got what they came for. Freedom. It's an important part of Boston tradition.

Of all the cities in the United States, Boston is in the upper ranks among places that are good for walking. For strollers, walkers, runners, joggers, even roller skaters, Boston is their kind of town. And one of the best walks in Boston is the one they call The Freedom Trail.

It begins at the Park Street side of the Common with a monument, not to the Revolutionary War, but to the Civil War; the Park Street Church. Henry James called it "the most interesting mass of brick and mortar in America." The call for the abolition of slavery went out from Boston first, and some of the most impassioned speeches were made from the pulpit here. Whether it was guilt over having made so much money in the slave trade or Puritan religious fervor, slavery was an issue all Boston responded to, and they were leaders both in the movement and in the war. Around the corner is the Old

Granary Burying Ground. It's one of five in the center of the city, and a favorite place for people who get their kicks making rubbings from old headstones. You need a permit to do it, but it's worth the effort because among some of the names the rubbers pick up are John Hancock, Samuel Adams and Mother Goose. Andrew Faneuil, of Faneuil Hall fame, is resting in peace under a stone inscribed with his nephew's first initial and his own name misspelled as "Funel." Benjamin Franklin's parents are buried there, too. So is Boston's very first mayor.

Why, you might ask, is a cemetery called a "granary." It was named for a huge shed that once stood next to it, built as a storehouse for surplus wheat and corn that could be distributed to the needy poor. But in the early days Boston had very few poor families and, after the custodian reported that "weevils have taken the wheat, and mice annoy the corn much, being very numerous," the building was torn down and the salvage used to build a tavern. But the name lives on, so to speak, in the cemetery.

The trail goes past the Athenaeum and into School Street, where colonial youngsters got a taste of 'the three Rs' and an occasional hickory stick at the Boston Latin School. At this point, strollers usually get a chance to sit down because the trail leads inside King's Chapel, the first Episcopal church in New England, but a Unitarian church since Revolutionary times, also the first of that denomination. Much of the furnishings consist of gifts from English royalty, and the interior can be called "Georgian" with no argument from anybody. In fact, it's probably the best example of Georgian decoration anywhere in New England.

The church was originally a wooden building, but was covered in local granite after the locals discovered it was a good building material. Once the stonework was finished, the old building was torn down from inside.

Not far away is the Old Corner Book Store, restored for us by yet another important Boston institution, the *Boston Globe*. Emerson knew the place well, so did Hawthorne and Longfellow. The old City Hall is there, too, wonderfully restored as a restaurant and office building. And not far from it, another great job of restoration, Old South Meetinghouse, now a bookstore and museum.

The Freedom Trail wanders past Faneuil Hall and the Quincy Market as well as the new City Hall, a massive pile of concrete and glazed brick. Then, mercifully, it takes you out of the way of an elevated expressway, a construction Boston seems to have in far too much abundance. And from there, it wanders back into the past for a look at the only wooden building left from the 17th century, Paul Revere's house. When it was built, it was conveniently located next to the town pump, across from the public market, near the meeting house, hard by the local guardhouse. A lively spot indeed. Paul Revere added some contributions to the general din; he had 16 children. He did a lot of things, too, of course. And his accomplishments are spread out for anyone who visits the house to see for themselves. The style of the house is Elizabethan English, and looks just like the homes the Puritans left behind in the old country. It also, of course, looks just like the houses they built when they got to Boston.

Most of the old houses were destroyed in a series of fires over the early years. Fire was surely their worst enemy, and it's the reason why very few authentic colonial buildings are left in any of the cities that were part of the original colonies. Urban "improvement" is another reason, too, of course. There isn't a single Dutch building left in New York, for instance. Most were destroyed by fire, but the last remaining one had an encounter with a wrecker's ball some years ago.

Just around the corner from Paul Revere's house, and an

appropriate end to the Freedom Trail, is Old North Church, where Paul Revere did his famous sound and light show. It's one of the oldest churches in Boston, with bells cast in England, and for years was the highest structure in the city, purposely made that way as a landmark for sailors. It looks a lot like the church of St. James in Piccadilly, London, and tourists in either direction usually notice the resemblance. Londoners with longer memories recognize it as a church that was once on Queen Victoria Street in London, called St. Andrews-by-the-Wardrobe with St. Anne, Blackfriars. Unfortunately, it was destroyed in the unpleasantness called the London Blitz. Some of the parishioners of North Church had come from Blackfriars, so the resemblance was more than a coincidence.

When it was built, it broke sharply with a tradition of long standing in New England. The Puritans had built meeting houses that were purposely simple, undecorative, uncomfortable. This church had a raised pulpit, galleries, divided pews and simple, but quite lovely, decoration. Popery? Some would have said so in 1723 when it was built. But by then the Puritans were ready for a little style on their religion.

We call it "Old" North Church today because of Longfellow's poem about Paul Revere's ride. Actually, it's the newer of two structures people called "North Church." The other one was chopped up for firewood by British troops billeted near there. And this one's official name is really Christ Church.

But it is old, and its style has been repeated in churches all over New England and up and down the East Coast. The steeple wasn't added until the church was more than 15 years old, but in plenty of time to be useful to Paul Revere. Like every other steeple in New England, it was built like a telescope from inside the church. As each stage got smaller, workmen's space got tighter. The spire, in this case a weather vane in the shape of a

flower and pot with a banner, a ball and five-pointed star, was built on the ground and then pushed up through the hole in the top. Life was much safer, if more confining, for steeplejacks in those days.

A hurricane blew the steeple down in 1804 and it was replaced, with one some 15 feet shorter than the original, by Charles Bulfinch. The same thing happened again in 1955, and it was replaced again. This time, they had to send all the way to New Hampshire for a crane high enough to replace the weather vane. So much for progress!

During the Revolution, the North End was a hotbed of Tories, and a great many of the residents left town and headed for Canada when they saw how things were turning out. Slightly deserted, the neighborhood got less fashionable and, anyway, people were beginning to long for the open spaces of the suburbs. They moved to Beacon Hill.

By the beginning of the 19th century, the North End had been converted from Boston's most prestigious neighborhood to a district of factories making everything from cannon balls to flower pots. The workers in the factories, because there was no subway then, moved into the neighborhood, and they were followed by new arrivals from abroad.

Within a generation the neighborhood would be called "Little Italy," and it's one of the most tightly-packed city neighborhoods anywhere in the United States. It's a section of narrow streets and alleys, tenement buildings with tomatoes and basil growing in pots on the fire escapes. Laundry flies from lines stretched between the buildings like the banners of some medieval festival. Old people, with lined faces you can't resist, sit outside their buildings discussing the past and the present, with their hands punctuating every sentence.

If you can make it past Quincy Market with your appetite intact, your reward is here. Stop in a groceria to take home a little homemade pasta as a souvenir of the trip. Go to a clam house for some scungilli, then next door to a trattoria for liguini, then on to a ristorante for the best veal cutlet limone this side of Naples. And for the crowning touch, sit in front of an outdoor café under a bright, red and green umbrella and sip hot and strong espresso while you watch this wonderful world pass by and treat yourself to a sinfully sweet cannoli.

Late in the summer and well into the fall, when most visitors to New England are heading for the hills to look for fall colors, the North East gets more colorful itself. It's fiesta time, and the streets are decorated with colored lights. The sidewalks are covered with stands selling pizza and ravioli, zeppole and Italian cheesecake. You can try your luck at games of chance or games of skill. And if you don't enjoy yourself, it's your problem.

The whole thing comes to a peak on October 12, when Boston Italians come out in force to remind other Bostonians that an Italian, Christopher Columbus, made it across the ocean in 1492, a long, long time before those Pilgrims set foot on Plymouth Rock in 1620.

After World War II, a great many younger Italian families moved away from the North End and out into the suburbs. But the neighborhood itself has a strong lure, and some are starting to come back now that areas around it are being renewed. And that's the best kind of urban renewal there is.

Italian Opera came to Boston some years after the Italians themselves. It started seriously with a performance of *La Gioconda* as the curtain raiser for the 1907 season. It was such a hit, the cultural establishment dispatched an architect to study all the great opera houses of Europe and to design a better one. Whether he succeeded or not is a matter for historians to debate. His opera house was torn down in 1958. But, while it lasted, it represented culture *par excellence* to Bostonians, who turned up each season dressed in the finest clothes and most expensive jewels their money could buy.

It should be mentioned, though, that opera may still be alive and well in Boston in the hands of Sarah Caldwell and her new Boston Opera.

The Puritans didn't have a passion for music, though some of them were known to be very good dancers. Their idea of a moving musical experience was an evening of psalm singing, and their idea of entertainment was listening to a good lecture. But in the mid 19th century, their mood changed as they discovered Mozart and lyric poetry, Haydn and great books. Forty years later, Henry Lee Higginson founded the Boston Symphony Orchestra. He directed it and supported it with his own money from its founding in 1881 until 1918.

In Boston, they call it simply "symphony." Boston women who want to be somebody meet their peers every Friday all winter long at the afternoon concerts in Symphony Hall. It's a ritual Lucius Beebe said takes on "the aspect of holy days dedicated to the classics and a vast craning of necks to be certain that the Hallowells and the Forbeses are in their accustomed stalls."

In summer "symphony" is at Tanglewood in the Berkshires, a tradition started by one of the orchestra's great conductors, Serge Koussevitzky, in 1936. The place he picked, which now also includes a summer music school, was the former summer home of Nathaniel Hawthorne.

For city-bound Bostonians, the Hatch Memorial

Bandshell on the Charles River is where to find the sounds of summer. All during the month of July, the Boston Pops entertains in free concerts there. It's a tradition, like the orchestra itself, begun by the late Arthur Fiedler, himself one of Boston's real treasures. The Pops Concerts are held inside Symphony Hall in the spring. But the real highlight of the year, for the Pops and for all of Boston is their Fourth of July concert on the river, complete with fireworks and their trademark, *The Stars and Stripes Forever.*

In summer, the grassy esplanade along the Charles River is a haven for joggers, sunbathers and lovers. At night, they stroll along Copley Plaza to listen to street musicians or sit on the steps of the Public Library to discuss among themselves what a wonderful place this city is. Or maybe they go down to the waterfront to pick up a breeze and a little wine and cheese.

Office workers spend their lunch hours on the plaza outside City Hall, grabbing a snack from a sidewalk vendor and relaxing to the sounds of a bluegrass fiddle or an electric piano, or both competing with each other.

It's always had the reputation of a livable city, but Boston may not have been more livable at any time in her history than right now. People who move there from other cities stay there. People who discover it as students keep going back to recharge their mental batteries. Quite simply, people who like cities love Boston.

It has its detractors, of course. What city doesn't? But people who find fault usually don't understand cities and don't care to. One of the most common comments you hear from them is that they aren't safe. Well, when someone asked the mayor of Boston if he wasn't worried about the possibility that places like Quincy Market might be a haven for purse-snatchers, he gave the answer the question deserved:

"If you're worried about handbag snatchers," he said, "you can live in the Berkshires."

And you'll never know what you're missing.

Previous page the Boston city skyline seen at night from Cambridge, across the Charles River.

This page the rounded dome and pillars of the First Church of Christ, Scientist, stand majestically amid the towering, high-rise buildings and the broad streets and expressways.

Opposite page the difference in scale between the houses of old Boston, on the far right of the picture, and the strident, modern architecture surrounding the area, is quite staggering.

Overleaf, left the statue of Joseph Hooker, Federal general in the Civil War (1861 – 1865). He was trained at West Point and served during the Mexican War (1846 – 1848). He participated in the major engagements of the Eastern campaigns and earned the nickname of 'Fighting Joe'. Although he successfully reorganized the Army of the Potomac in early 1863, he was outmaneuvered and defeated by Robert E. Lee at the Battle of Chancellorsville (May 1 – 4, 1863). He resigned his command when he felt that Washington no longer trusted his capability. However, on November 24, 1863, he won the 'Battle Above the Clouds' on Lookout Mountain, which cleared the way for Federal success on Missionary Ridge.

Overleaf, right:
Top left the soaring, mirror-like structure of the John Hancock Tower.
Top right the New Boston City Hall which was designed by architects Kallman, McKinnell and Knowles. When it was opened in 1969 there was much controversy, its critics calling it an 'Aztec Tomb'.
Bottom left the tranquil scene near Commercial Wharf, with boats riding peacefully at their moorings.
Bottom right the Sheraton Boston Hotel and the 52-floor Prudential Center amid the skyscraper surrounds of Boston.

These pages homeward-bound cars leave iridescent trails
along the streets and bridges of the city. Dusk gives
way to night and buildings blaze with myriad points of
light, while parks lie deserted, their snowy covering
stained by the fluorescent glow.

This page crisscrossed with paths, Boston Common – bordered by Beacon Street to the left and Tremont Street to the right – is the oldest public park in the country. *Opposite page* the magnificent, broad sweep of the Charles River.

Opposite page **a glittering array of lights illuminates the city at night.** *This page* **countless pleasure craft ply the waters of the Charles River. Boston Harbor is, of course, another stretch of water for the sailing enthusiast.**

This page dominating Beacon Hill is the Massachusetts State House, with its golden dome. Charles Bulfinch designed the central brick portion and, in 1795, Governor Samuel Adams, aided by Paul Revere, laid the cornerstone. *Opposite page* marina on the Charles River.

These pages the First Church of Christ, Scientist, is
the world headquarters of the Christian Science Church.
Founded by Mary Baker Eddy in 1879 to 'reinstate
primitive Christianity and its element of healing', the
building is set within a modern center designed by Pei.

This page the city is seen, glowing golden in the rays of the setting winter sun, across the Charles River which is packed with ice. *Opposite page* a replica ship, the brig *Beaver II*, recalls the historic Boston Tea Party incident.

Previous pages the waterfront area of Boston contains several noteworthy reminders of its historical past. The brig *Beaver II* is an authentic replica of one of the three ships involved in the Boston Tea Party. The other tall ship, with its cannon run out, is the *U.S.S. Constitution.* Known as 'Old Ironsides' because of the cannon balls which had bounced off her during a naval engagement, she was restored in 1833. *These pages* the bustling city scene.

This page, bottom left **Boston City Hall.** *Bottom right* **North Station.** *Right* **Old South Meeting House. This was built as a Congregational church in 1729 and was intended to be more liberal than the older Puritan churches. Before the Revolution, many meetings were held in the Old South because of the small size of the original Faneuil Hall. On December 16, 1773, Josiah Quincy and Samuel Adams spoke to a group of several thousand. When it was known that the Governor, Hutchinson, was not going to change his position with regard to the landing of tea, men from the Sons of Liberty headed for the riverfront to stage their protest.**

Opposite page **the First Church of Christ, Scientist.**

Opposite page **New England Aquarium and Long Wharf.** *This page, above* **the ship** *Beaver II* **at the Boston Tea Party Museum recalls that historic day when a group of 'Indians' gathered together at Griffin's Wharf.**

They then proceeded to systematically break open chests of tea, spilling the contents into the waters of the Harbor. *Right and top right* **the frigate** *U.S.S. Constitution,* **laid down in 1794.**

These pages scenes along the Charles River and in the Harbor area. *Right* the bowsprit of the brig *Beaver II*. The original ship was at the center of the Boston Tea Party on December 16, 1773, when rebellious American colonists threw a cargo of tea into the waters of the Harbor.

The Tea Act of April 1773 revised a tax upon what was then one of the country's best-loved drinks, and was therefore resented by all. It became a focus for discontent and when, in retaliation for the incident in Boston Harbor, the British Parliament passed the 'Intolerable Acts', the stage was set for revolution. One of Parliament's first actions was to introduce the Boston Port Bill, to close the port to trade until payment had been made for the tea.

This page the Boston skyline at dusk. Beneath the proud
bulk of the tall buildings, cars on the John F.
Fitzgerald Expressway leave trails of red and white.
Opposite page in contrast, at dawn, the pale light of
the sun is reflected from the John Hancock Tower.

Opposite page **the Back Bay area.** *This page* **the First Church of Christ, Scientist. Christian Science is the name given by Mary Baker Eddy (1821 – 1910) to a religious system which she evolved, in which matter is declared unreal and God or Mind infinite.**

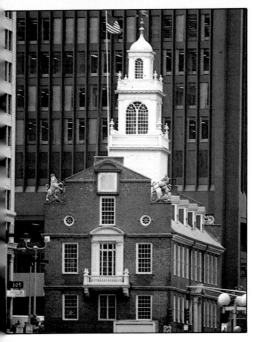

Opposite page, top left and bottom right **Beacon Hill;** *top right, bottom left and this page, top* **Copp's Hill Burying Ground.** *Right* **statue of Paul Revere.** *Far right* **Granary Burying Ground.** *Above* **Old State House.**

This page, top left the State House as seen from Boston Common. Inside can be found the Hall of Flags, which contains the original battle flags that were carried by Massachusetts troops. In the State Senate Chamber hangs the Sacred Cod. Made of hand-carved pine, it is the emblem of the state's early source of wealth. Davy Crockett referred to it by saying that it 'was quite natural to me, for at home I have at one end of my house the antlers of a noble buck and the heavy paws of a bear'. *Left* Massachusetts Institute of Technology from the air. *Above* the Custom House Tower from Marine Park. *Opposite page* First Church of Christ, Scientist.

Opposite page, top left and bottom left the
First Church of Christ, Scientist. *Top right* the
Old South Meeting Place. *Bottom right* **King's
Chapel.** *This page, above* the **Old South Church.**
Top and right **Trinity Church.**

Opposite page **the Senate Chamber of the State House.** *This page, above* **the Museum of Fine Arts.** *Right* **Marine Park and the Custom House Tower.** *Top left* **Fort Point Channel.** *Top right* **the Christian Science Center.**

This page **Cambridge and the Charles River as seen from the air.** *Opposite page* **aerial view over Harvard University – which was founded in 1636 and is the oldest institution of higher education in the country – to Downtown Boston.**

This page **shades of purple stain the city panorama as dusk gives way to night, while bright lights from man's structures bravely shine out across the Charles River.** *Opposite page* **within the Public Gardens stands the illuminated statue of George Washington by Thomas Ball.**

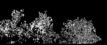

This page **the light-flecked shapes of the skyscrapers are reflected back from the surface of the Charles River.** *Opposite page* **the gilded dome of the State House overlooks the old residential area from its lofty perch on Beacon Hill.**

This page **Boston's history is inextricably linked to the sea. Much of its early prosperity was made through trade using the old clipper ships as transport.**
Opposite page **the State House. Although designed in 1795 by Charles Bulfinch, it was only in 1861 that the gold-leaf work was added to the dome. Within can be found the Archives Museum which contains the Massachusetts Constitution, the oldest written constitution in the world still in effect. Its preamble states, 'The end of the institution, maintainence, and administration of government, is to secure the existence of the body politic, to protect it, and to furnish the individuals who compose it, with the power of enjoying in safety and tranquility their natural rights, and blessing of life...' Governor Bradford's *Of Plimoth Plantation* is also there. It is a record of the Pilgrims from their time in England right through their initial period in America. It disappeared during the Revolution and was believed lost forever. However, although nobody knows how it got there, over a hundred years later it surfaced in the Bishop of London's library!**

Previous pages, left **the lantern of Trinity Church;** *right* **the House of Representatives in the State House.** *This page, top left* **the John Hancock Tower.** *Above* **the Charles River at dusk.** *Remaining pictures* **lamplight illuminations.** *Opposite page* **the First Church of Christ, Scientist.**

Previous pages **panoramic views of Boston.** *This page, top left* **the famous Swan Boats in the Public Gardens.** *Above* **the Old State House.**

Remaining pictures and opposite page **scenes around Quincy Market, built in 1826 under the direction of the mayor at that time, Josiah Quincy.**

Previous pages, left **the glorious tulips which grow in the lovely Public Garden.** *Previous pages, right* **now known as Faneuil Hall Marketplace, the market was conceived by Mayor Josiah Quincy and opened on August 26, 1826. The three 500-foot-long buildings were designed by architect Alexander Parris. The South Market was reopened on August 26, 1977, and the North Market exactly one year later.**

This page, top left **opposite the State House stands the monument to Robert Gould Shaw (1837 – 1863), the army officer who commanded the 54th Massachusetts, the first regiment of black troops in the Federal forces during the Civil War. He was eventually killed in action.** *Left* **a Swan Boat in the Public Gardens.** *Above and opposite page, bottom left* **the statue of George Washington, also in the Public Gardens.**

Opposite page, top right **the steps outside the State House.** *Top left* **the Soldiers and Sailors Monument on Boston Common.** *Remaining photographs* **the Annual Loyalty Day Program is held on Boston Common each May Day. On these occasions, the Ladies Auxiliary to the Veterans of Foreign Wars of the United States rededicate their allegiance to liberty and justice.**

These pages, left **a shop in the Charles Street area.** Remaining photographs **Faneuil Hall Marketplace. The Hall's second floor is a meeting place of which Hack wrote, 'Here Orators in ages past have mounted their attack/Undaunted by proximity of sausage on the rack.'**

Previous pages **colorful Haymarket and Chinatown.** *This page* **the city looking east across Back Bay.** *Opposite page* **Boston Common is the oldest public park in the country, dating from 1634. Here witches have been hanged and 'common scolds' dunked in the Frog Pond.**

This page **the Charles River and the Back Bay area.**
Opposite page **the Red Sox's stadium at Fenway Park.**

This page from September through May, the educational establishments of Boston supplement the city's professional sporting fixtures. One of the best known teams is that of Harvard University and seen here are football players from their team during a match at Harvard Stadium.

Opposite page the Red Sox baseball team, shown playing on their home ground at Fenway Park. Boston is rightly proud of its sporting heroes and there are always enthusiastic crowds of spectators at their fixtures.

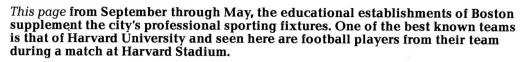

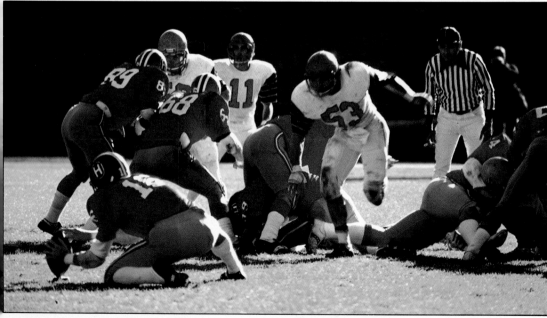

This page, top left **Orchard House** and *top right* **The Wayside, Concord.** *Left* **Buckman Tavern, Lexington,** was the meeting point for minutemen on the day of battle. Here, Captain Parker ordered his men, trying to stop the British march on Concord, 'Stand your ground, don't fire unless fired upon, but if they mean to have a war let it begin here'. *Above* **Longfellow's Wayside Inn, Sudbury.** *Opposite page* **Longfellow House, Cambridge.**

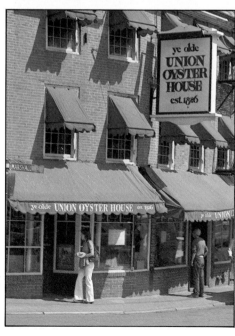

These pages the houses on Beacon Hill reflect the Federal and Greek revival styles of late 18th to mid-19th centuries. The area's name evolved from the order of the General Court in 1634, 'There shalbe forthwith a beacon sett on the sentry hill att Boston, to give notice to the country of any danger.'

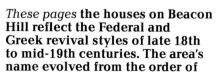

This page, left **Lowell House, Harvard University.** The bells came from the Danilov Monastery, Russia. A bell-tuner came too and began to tune them by filing the rims, but President Lowell stopped him, thinking he was damaging the bells. The Russian began to believe that he was being persecuted and poisoned, so he started to drink ink as an antidote! Lowell sent him home and Harvard's maintenance man tried tuning the bells himself. *Above* **Smith Halls.** *Opposite page* **University Hall,** designed by Bulfinch in 1816. The inscription on the statue in front reads 'John Harvard, Founder, 1638'. It is known as the 'Statue of Three Lies': the college was founded in 1636; Harvard was a benefactor, not the founder, and nobody knows what Harvard looked like.

These pages **North Bridge, Concord. Minutemen met the British here on April 19, 1775. Emerson has immortalized the skirmish in the** *Concord Hymn* **in which he wrote of 'the shot heard round the world'.**

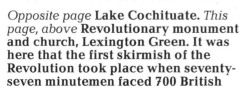

Opposite page **Lake Cochituate.** *This page, above* **Revolutionary monument and church, Lexington Green.** It was here that the first skirmish of the Revolution took place when seventy-seven minutemen faced 700 British soldiers. The latter's first volley killed 8 and wounded 10. *Top center* **the Minuteman Statue.** *Top right* **Indian statue outside the Museum of Fine Arts.** *Right* **Martha Mary's Chapel near the Wayside Inn, Sudbury.**

Opposite page **Faneuil Hall Marketplace.** *This page* **Old Granary Burial Ground. In the center of the picture is the grave of Benjamin Franklin's parents. Also buried here are John Hancock, Samuel Adams and Robert Paine, three signatories of the Declaration of Independence.**

Opposite page, top left **Boston Common;** *bottom left* **Copp's Hill Burying Ground.** *This page, right* **Boston Public Library.** *Remaining pictures* **Paul Revere House and statue.**

These pages **the brownstone buildings of Beacon Hill are now contained in an area preserved as a National Historic Landmark. The sidewalks are still made of brick, and at night gaslight lamps maintain the essential atmosphere of this architectural delight.**

Opposite page, top left **the Public Gardens and its Swan Boats** *bottom left.* **Bottom right the statue of Washington;** *top right* **Trinity Church.** *This page, top left* **Copp's Hill Burying Ground.** *Top center* **Old West Church.** *Remaining pictures* **Beacon Hill.**

This page, top left **Beacon Street.**
Bottom left **Louisburg Square.** *Top right* **Charles Street Meeting House.**
Bottom right **numbers 11, 13 and 15**

Chestnut Street. *Opposite page* **the courtyard of the Isabella Stewart Gardner Museum, which houses a fine art and furniture collection.**

These pages **Harvard University is the oldest and one of the foremost academic institutions in the United States. Famous literary graduates include Ralph Waldo Emerson, Henry James, and Robert Frost. The university developed the Harvard classification system for stars. It also produced several U.S. Presidents, including Theodore Roosevelt, Franklin D. Roosevelt, and John F. Kennedy. The white-spired building is that of Memorial Church, dedicated to the men from Harvard who were killed during two World Wars. The Doric columns of its portico were made in a shipyard because of their size.** *Opposite page, bottom left* **the Science Center, designed by Jose Luis Sert and Associates.** *This page, top* **the Alexander Calder Stabile.**

This page **the dome of the Massachusetts Institute of Technology rises above the Charles River. Chartered in 1861, it opened in Boston in 1865 and moved to Cambridge in 1916. Facilities include a nuclear reactor and nuclear engineering laboratory.** *Opposite page* **Harvard Yard, Harvard University.**

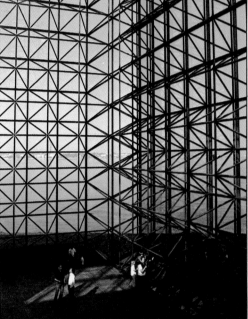

This page opened in 1980, the John F. Kennedy Library pays tribute to the late President's administration. *Opposite page* the Main Hall of the Museum of Science. Contained within this building are exhibits from the worlds of natural history, physical science, medicine, astronomy and the new frontier – outer space.

Boston's history is the history of the American Revolution. Its future lies within the same framework of ideals based on freedom and justice.